Greg Germann, Colette Kilroy, Marylouise Burke, Matthew Lewis, and Susan Knight in a scene from the New York production of "Apocalyptic Butterflies." The set was designed by Nephelie Andonyadis.

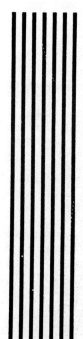

APOCALYPTIC
BUTTERFLIES

By
WENDY MACLEOD

**DRAMATISTS
PLAY SERVICE
INC.**

APOCALYPTIC BUTTERFLIES was presented by New Arts Theatre Company (Joshua Astrachan, Artistic Director) at the INTAR Hispanic American Theatre in New York City on June 3, 1989. The play was directed by Marcus Stern; the set design was by Nephelie Andonyadis; the costume design was by Melina Root; the lighting design was by Scott Zielinski; the sound design was by John Huntington; the music was composed by Marcus Stern; and the production stage manager was James Mountcastle. The cast was as follows:

HANK TATER	Greg Germann
MURIEL	Colette Kilroy
FRANCINE	Marylouise Burke
DICK	Matthew Lewis
TRUDI	Susan Knight

APOCALYPTIC BUTTERFLIES was presented by The Immediate Theatre Company in Chicago, Illinois in November 1988. The play was directed by Jeff Ginsberg; the set design was by Maggie Bodwell; the costume design was by Anne Jaros; the lighting design was by Peter Gottlieb; the sound design was by David Naunton; and the production stage manager was Joan Foster McCarty. The cast was as follows:

HANK TATER	Paul Raci
MURIEL	Peggy Goss
FRANCINE	Millie McManus
DICK	Bradley Mott
TRUDI	Joan Schwenk

APOCALYPTIC BUTTERFLIES was presented by Yale Repertory Theatre (Lloyd Richards, Artistic Director; Benjamin Mordecai, Managing Director) as part of Winterfest 7, in New Haven, Connecticut in January 1987. The play was directed by Richard Hamburger; the set design was by E. David Cosier, Jr.; the costume design was by Phillip R. Baldwin; the lighting design was by Tim Saternow; and the stage manager was Neal Fox. The cast was as follows:

HANK TATER . . . . Steven Skybell
MURIEL . . . . Tessie Hogan
FRANCINE. . . . . DeAnn Mears
DICK. . . . . Frank Hamilton
TRUDI. . . . . Susan Gibney

APOCALYPTIC BUTTERFLIES premiered at the Magic Theatre (John Lion, General Director) in San Francisco, California in November 1987. The play was directed by Julie Hébert; the set design was by John Mayne; the costume design was by Regina Cate; the lighting design was by Novella Smith; the sound design was by Earwax Productions; and the stage manager was Christina J. Moore. The cast was as follows:

HANK TATER. . . . . Mark Petrakis
MURIEL. . . . . Kathleen Cramer
FRANCINE. . . . . Priscilla Alden
DICK. . . . . Morgan Upton
TRUDI. . . . . Karen Hott

CHARACTERS

Hank Tater
Muriel *his wife*
Francine *his mother*
Dick *his father*
Trudi

SETTING

Fryeburg, Maine

Hank and Muriel's kitchen, a motel room, Dick and Francine's trailer home, a field in front of a totem pole.

TIME

Christmas time

December 23, 24, and 25

APOCALYPTIC BUTTERFLIES

SCENE 1

A kitchen. Red checked curtains. An empty baby carriage. A pot-bellied stove with L.L. Bean boots and car batteries around it. A hook by the door strewn with rain ponchos and mittens. A string of blinking Christmas lights hangs over a window. Hank is wearing a red ragg wool sweater and boxer shorts, with red ragg wool socks. Muriel, wearing a flannel nightgown is fixing breakfast. Hank, agitated, walks to the door and looks out.

HANK. Can you believe this? Can you believe this? *(Hank smacks the table.)* I cannot BELIEVE this. *(Muriel serves a plate.)*

MURIEL. Sit down and eat.

HANK. What the hell is this?

MURIEL. You know perfectly well what it is. It's a poached egg.

HANK. *(Pushing the plate away in disgust.)* It got my toast all wet. *(Hank pushes back his chair and gets up.)* I'm gonna call him.

MURIEL. Hank, it was a gift.

HANK. I'm gonna get him on the horn. *(Dialing.)* First he starts with the rocks.

MURIEL. Well not exactly rocks, Hank. Sacred sites...

HANK. Yeah, I got your sacred sites ... shit. Busy. *(Hank hangs up.)*

MURIEL. You'd be surprised, Hank, a lot of people go for rocks

7

in a big way. He might sell some of those paintings.

HANK. Who? WHO goes for rocks in a big way? Painting pictures of fucking Stonehenge. Now listen to me, Muriel, listen to me on this point. Whatever you think of Stonehenge, I mean whatever you or I or your man in the street thinks about Stonehenge, it is already a thing. A thing in and of itself. A work of art. So what is the point of painting a picture of a work of art. It redundants itself. It's like painting a picture of the Mona Lisa. It's stupid, it's ridiculous. I'm gonna call him. *(Hank goes for the phone. He steps in a puddle.)* What the hell is this?

MURIEL. Well you're walking around in your stocking feet.

HANK. I've got Lake fucking Ontario on my kitchen floor.

MURIEL. It's from the boots, the snow on the boots. Get a paper towel. *(Hank holds a paper towel against his socks while he hops to the door.)*

HANK. Look at this, would you look at this. I sweated for that lawn last summer. It's not easy having a lawn in the country. Every time you turn your back ferns are creeping towards the house. They're like from another planet those ferns — I told you about the ferns in the car thing. I fucking leave my car windows open one night. ONE NIGHT. The next day ferns are sprouting out of the upholstery.

MURIEL. Hank, about the fern thing...

HANK. What?

MURIEL. Ferns were growing out of the upholstery, okay, but...

HANK. But <u>what?</u>

MURIEL. It was not overnight. You left the Falcon on blocks all winter and in the spring you found a fern growing there. *(Pause.)*

HANK. I'm gonna call him.

MURIEL. Oh Hank, it can't kill the lawn, we don't even have a lawn, all we have is snow. And then we have snow. And in the spring we have mud and after the mud is when we think about the lawn so don't get pissed off about the lawn thing.

HANK. *(Dialing.)* Six two or two six?

8

MURIEL. I'm not telling you.

HANK. Six two or two six Muriel?

MURIEL. It was his surprise for your birthday, Henry.

HANK. FOUR THOUSAND DOLLARS WORTH OF TO-TEM POLES! DUMPED ON MY FRONT LAWN!

MURIEL. IT WAS A GIFT!

HANK. YEAH WELL HE SHOULDN'T HAVE! *(A baby cries offstage.)* Oh yeah, here we go. *(Muriel exits.)* Where the hell did he get 4,000 dollars! And the question on all of our minds — where did he find that many totem poles? *(Muriel re-enters.)*

MURIEL. *(Softly.)* He belongs to a club.

HANK. WHAT?

MURIEL. A totem pole club. Keep your voice down. May I ask you a question?

HANK. No.

MURIEL. Why is it whenever she cries I have to go in to her? You're standing right here, you're the one who made her cry. She's your daughter too, but I go in. What is that?

HANK. I really need this right now, Muriel, I really need this.

MURIEL. Okay, so you didn't like your gift. Okay. Just remember it's the thought that counts.

HANK. Living with you is like living with a Chinese philosopher or something, "it's the thought that counts," gee, that's kind of a fresh take on the whole situation.

MURIEL. Do you know I don't even enjoy talking to you anymore? Sometimes I think about my old boyfriend. He was unique. He read me Winnie-the-Pooh books.

HANK. Yeah, but you didn't love him the way you wanted to love a man, that's what you told me.

MURIEL. We had conversations. He respected my opinions. He wasn't just some Mister Man.

HANK. Are you saying I'm just some Mister Man?

MURIEL. Maybe you're not all that unusual, that's all.

HANK. Are you telling me a man with 4,000 dollars worth of totem poles is not unusual? Because if you're telling me that I'm not staying in this house!

MURIEL. *(Sniffling.)* Stop yelling at me.

HANK. Ah baby. *(Hank crosses to her. He is standing and she is sitting. She puts her arms around his waist. He smooths down her hair.)*

MURIEL. It's <u>Christmastime.</u>

HANK. I know. What am I gonna get you, huh? What do you want for Christmas?

MURIEL. A compliment.

HANK. Yeah?

MURIEL. Yeah.

HANK. You make me feel honored. I feel honored being married to you. I ever told you that?

MURIEL. No.

HANK. I don't deserve you.

MURIEL. Yes you do.

HANK. Sometimes. Sometimes I do.

MURIEL. Hey, do you know what your underwear says?

HANK. What?

MURIEL. It gives like phony translations for French phrases. Like Jeanne d'Arc is translated as a bathroom with the light out.

HANK. What'd you do that for? We were getting intimate. We were embracing each other. We were soothing each other. I was smoothing down your cowlick with affection and you get jokey with me.

MURIEL. I was just trying to make you laugh. To make you forget about the totem poles.

HANK. Fuck! The totem poles. What am I gonna do? We look like a trading post or something. Where's the piece of paper, where's the receipt thing? I'm gonna call these totem pole assholes, tell them to get their buns over here and get these fucking artifacts out of my yard.

MURIEL. Do you think they're really artifacts? Do you think they're the real thing?

HANK. As opposed to what?

MURIEL. Reproductions. Made in some factory.

HANK. Totem pole factories?

MURIEL. Well I don't know. Who do YOU think made them?

HANK. Whoever the hell makes 'em should find another job because that's a hell of a stupid thing to waste your life on.

MURIEL. To the Indians it's a religious thing. It's like a crucifix to us.

HANK. Same difference. I'm not prejudiced. I'd be just as pissed I had 4,000 dollars worth of crucifixes in my front yard. Whatever happened to that idol commandment? That false idol thing. *(Hank finds the receipt. He cradles the phone between his ear and shoulder and dials.)* I tell you what. The 4,000 dollars I could have used. Could a got a valve job on the VW. And rustoleum on the bottom. I'm like Fred Flintstone in that thing. I drive through a puddle, whoosh up through the bottom of the car all over my pants.

Hello? Yeah. This Acme trucking? It's about the totem pole products you delivered this morning to the Lake Road, Tater residence. Yeah, yeah, hang on... *(He reads from the delivery receipt.)* 2-4-1-7-8-G-X. Yeah. He's checking. They're playing fucking "Raindrops Keep Falling on My Head." I really need this right now.

Acme. That was in the roadrunner cartoon. You know everytime a delivery came from Acme, KABOOM somebody blows.

MURIEL. I hated that cartoon.

HANK. WHAT? No, you're kidding. Don't tell me you hated Roadrunner because it was violent because that's just obvious. That's an obvious sentiment.

MURIEL. I didn't like that Roadrunner, I didn't like his attitude.

HANK. His?

MURIEL. What?

HANK. You said his. See I always thought Roadrunner was a woman. Funny, huh? You say tomato and I say fucking tomato. *(To the phone.)* Yo! Right here. Wo, wo, wo, whattdya mean you have no record? It was this morning. They're outside my window. I'm looking at 'em. And don't blame it on the fucking computer. I've had it with this computer crap. What do you mean you don't have a computer! Get on the stick, babies. Welcome to the 21st Century! Look, the name's Hank Tater, 876-2135, you track down that order and then you retract it. Capeesh? *(Hank hangs up.)*

MURIEL. This isn't the 21st century.

HANK. What?

MURIEL. You said Welcome to the 21st Century. On the phone. Just now.

HANK. I was irate.

MURIEL. So?

HANK. When a man is irate he does not have time to proofread his conversation. Just stop picking with me, okay? I gotta get to the shoe outlet.

MURIEL. Tonight's the night.

HANK. Yeah, yeah, yeah.

MURIEL. I'm not nagging you. I'm telling you. I'm reminding you.

HANK. I'm not looking forward to seeing that fruitcake.

MURIEL. He's not a fruitcake. He's your father.

HANK. You know fruitcakes? Who likes those? Who invented those? I don't recognize any of the fruit they put in there.

MURIEL. I like fruitcake.

HANK. JESUS CHRIST MURIEL!

MURIEL. <u>What?</u>

HANK. Can't you just agree with me? Can't you just agree with me on something — cartoons, fruitcakes, anything. Be nice to me. Be sweet to me. I need ... some sweetness in my life.

MURIEL. Look Hank, before you go, we got to talk about naming this baby.

HANK. I don't have time, I gotta get to the shoe store.

MURIEL. I made a list of possibilities. I bought a book.

HANK. A name book.

MURIEL. Yeah, a name book.

HANK. You think you can just pull a name out of a book, smack it on a baby and have it stick? A name's gotta mean something, a name's gotta have meaning.

MURIEL. They list the meanings right here in the book. Like — "Elvira, of German-Spanish extraction, meaning elf-counsel."

HANK. Elf-counsel. What the hell is that?

MURIEL. Well, I don't know.

HANK. I don't like Elvira, whatever the hell it means. It won't wash at Fryeburg Elementary, I know that.

MURIEL. THAT'S your criteria? Whether or not it'll wash at puny little nothing nowhere Fryeburg Elementary?

HANK. Whatever's up your ass don't take it out on Fryeburg Elementary alright? Because you're treading on my private and personal associations.

MURIEL. Listen, Hank, I got a whole list here so you don't have to jump on me every time you hate a name. *(Reading.)* "Lorelei. Mythological. The Lorelei were sirens of the river Rhine. Alluring."

HANK. The hell with alluring. Alluring means pregnant in high school, that's what alluring means, who needs the aggravation?

MURIEL. *(Reading.)* "Jessica, meaning wealthy."

HANK. That's a hot one. Let's not be ironical.

MURIEL. *(Reading.)* "Velvet, meaning velvety."

HANK. How much you spend on this book?

MURIEL. $2.95, Hank. I threw caution to the wind, I said what the hell, I owe it to myself, you only live once, I'll live on oatmeal if I have to but I have to have that book!

HANK. Don't get sarcastic. It was a legitimate query.

MURIEL. You're always digging at me, how it's your money, your credit cards.

HANK. It is my money. I earn it. At my job. Where I go with enormous loathing 5 days a week.

MURIEL. What am I some kind of indentured servant?

HANK. Right. Muriel, meaning "pitiful existence." Hey, they got boy names in there?

MURIEL. You're not giving my daughter a boy name.

HANK. Look up Hank.

MURIEL. Your real name's Henry.

HANK. Look up Hank!

MURIEL. All right. *(Reading.)* "Hank, see Henry."

HANK. *(Grabbing the book.)* Gimme that. "Heath, Hector, Henderson, Henry... Old German, meaning 'ruler of an estate.' " I got an idea. Let's make a list of the multitudinous other things you could have bought with $2.95.

MURIEL. Look Hank, we gotta name this baby. She's seven weeks old, she's overdue for a Christening. Until this baby is baptized she's in very serious danger of going to Limbo.

HANK. Say's who?

MURIEL. Everybody. The rules.

HANK. I don't want our baby should go to Limbo.

MURIEL. Me neither Hank.

HANK. I'm gonna cooperate in order to speed up this process. *(Reading.)* "Chanda, Chandra, Chantal, Chelsea, Cher, Cherie, Cherry, Chiquita, Cinderella, meaning 'little one of the ashes.' " This is like a book of names for babies born in California. I want an American name that means something to somebody around here. I want an American name that a substitute teacher can pronounce.

MURIEL. We could name her after your mother.

HANK. Francine. No offense to Ma, but it sounds like the name of a woman who works in a diner.

MURIEL. Your mother did work in a diner.

HANK. That's why I got the association. Look Muriel, I gotta get to the shoe outlet, but what I suggest you do is pull out the phone book, have a look-see 'cause those are all names that exist in the state of Maine. *(Hank glances out the window at the totem poles.)* Hey Muriel?

MURIEL. Yeah Hank?

HANK. I think they're getting closer.

BLACKOUT

14

SCENE TWO

*Francine, Dick, Muriel, and Hank sit around a half-eaten
birthday cake. Dick is wearing an old-fashioned yellow slicker
and smoking a pipe.*

MURIEL. Pebbles in his face?

DICK. Pebbles. Three pebbles embedded in his face. Here and
here and here.

FRANCINE. What blew up exactly?

DICK. A snow machine. At the ski resort over to Moss Ridge.

HANK. Don't do that down East crap. That over to Moss Ridge
crap. Say at. The ski resort at Moss Ridge.

MURIEL. And then what happened, Dick?

DICK. Okay, so they drove down to Mass. General and found out
it would cost thousands of dollars to have them removed and he'd
have to spend 10 days in the hospital. So ... they just left them
in.

HANK. Bullshit.

DICK. Only thing is he nicks himself while shaving.

HANK. Total bullshit.

FRANCINE. Muriel, this cake is delicious. She made your cake
from scratch, Hank.

HANK. It tastes good. Sweet.

MURIEL. Too sweet?

HANK. No, like cake sweet.

MURIEL. It's your favorite. With the coconut.

FRANCINE. It tastes good, huh?

HANK. Ma, I said it tastes good. It tastes good, Muriel.

MURIEL. You don't have to lie, Hank, if...

15

HANK. It's GOOD. It tastes good.

DICK. Your mother and I are doing the Christmas pageant this year.

MURIEL. What pageant?

HANK. It's not a <u>pageant.</u>

FRANCINE. Well no, it's not exactly a pageant. It's kind of a picture with people in it. They set up a little stable and the Ryans lend a few farm animals and we wear costumes and people walk by.

DICK. Your mother promised we wouldn't have any lines.

FRANCINE. We have one, we have exactly one line.

DICK. I keep forgetting it I got a glitch in my gray matter.

FRANCINE. Well get out your slip of paper, Dick, I put it on a slip of paper for ya. *(Dick finds the slip of paper in his raincoat pocket then methodically puts on his eyeglasses.)*

DICK. *(Reading.)* And are come to worship him.

HANK. That don't make any sense. It begins with an "and."

FRANCINE. That's cause I say the first part. Dick, you remember, I say, "For we have seen his star in the East," then you say... *(Pause.)*

DICK. Hang on. Lemme get my glasses. *(Dick methodically reaches for his glasses.)*

HANK. I hope you're wearing a warm costume 'cause you're gonna freeze sitting out there.

FRANCINE. Well Hank, we don't sit out there all day, just for a half hour before services.

DICK. So Hank, how's it feel to be a year older?

HANK. I'm not a year older, I'm a day older. I'm a day older than I was yesterday so I'm not going through any big transitional period here.

DICK. Sounds like it don't feel too good.

HANK. No Dad, it don't feel too good having your house look like a souvenir stand.

DICK. Those aren't souvenirs, son, those are the real thing. Lotta power in those totem poles, lotta protection. This house is protected.

HANK. I don't feel protected, I feel smothered. There's so many

16

G. D. totem poles this house don't get any sun. After all the clearing I did last fall, clearing out those bushes and ferns and shit.

DICK. Those ferns are something, huh?

HANK. I'm telling ya. So what I'm saying Dad is ... I reject your birthday gift.

DICK. I understand that.

HANK. You do?

DICK. Ayup.

HANK. Don't say "ayup!" God, you're trying to be like a New England calendar or something. You're turning yourself into a cartoon. What are ya wearing that slicker for? That's for the ocean, if you're a fisherman or something, you ran a hardware store.

DICK. I don't want to disappoint the tourists. They come on pilgrimages hoping to hear and see certain images they got in their heads.

HANK. They don't go on pilgrimages, they go on vacations. They smell the pine needles, eat a lobster, complain the water's too cold and go home. They're not your responsibility, you can take the slicker off.

FRANCINE. I like the raincoat. I can locate him on the property.

HANK. I can't stand yellow. I can't even look at yellow. Nothing good in nature is yellow.

MURIEL. Butter.

HANK. Cholesterol.

MURIEL. You eat it.

DICK. Where's that baby of yours?

HANK. Baby?

MURIEL. In the bedroom.

HANK. Oh God, baby. I didn't hear what you said, I mean I did but for a second I forgot we had one.

MURIEL. *(Exiting.)* I'll get her.

DICK. What are you gonna name that baby?

HANK. I don't know, we got twelve name books floating around the house. Muriel has come up with some doozies that needed rejection fast. *(Muriel re-enters holding the baby.)*

17

MURIEL. Here she is.

FRANCINE. *(Sing-song.)* There she is!

DICK. Gimme the little pisspot!

MURIEL. Let me know when she needs a diapering. *(Dick holds the baby and sings.)*

DICK. Stinky in the morning
      Stinky in the afternoon
      Stinky in the evening
      Stinky by the light of the moon.

HANK. What the hell kind of lullaby is that?

DICK. An original Dick Tater composition.

HANK. What the hell kind of song is that for an infant baby?

MURIEL. It's just a song.

HANK. Telling it it's stinky, singing about bodily functions.

MURIEL. There's nothing wrong with bodily functions.

HANK. That's not what you told me last night.

MURIEL. Hank.

DICK. What did Muriel give you for your birthday, Hank?

HANK. An axe.

DICK. This it here?

HANK. Yeah.

DICK. Oh it's a beaut, Muriel.

MURIEL. Hank picked it out. Also a shirt, he's wearing it.

FRANCINE. Nice.

HANK. I picked it out too.

DICK. Hold the baby son, the baby wants her Daddy.

HANK. That baby does not want her Daddy, that baby don't give a shit about her Daddy.

MURIEL. Listen to the way you're talking Hank, and you won't let your father sing a little stinky song.

DICK. Take the baby, son.

HANK. No, I haven't had any practice. Muriel won't let me hold it, she thinks I'll drop it or something.

MURIEL. I didn't think you wanted to hold it, Hank, and stop calling her an "it." She's a her.

FRANCINE. This baby needs a name. When this baby is named she won't be an it or a her, she'll be a somebody.

18

DICK. Here son, take the baby. Just support her head.

HANK. No, I don't want to, she'll cry.

FRANCINE. She won't cry.

HANK. She will. She does. She always cries I come near. *(Dick places the child in Hank's arms. The baby wails. Hank looks down at his shirt disbelieving.)* She puked on me. She waited till she got to me then puked on me.

MURIEL. Not on purpose.

HANK. She got puke all over my new shirt. I buy maybe exactly one shirt a year and it gets puked on the first day I wear it. The first day I wear it, it gets puked on!

MURIEL. It didn't look that great on you anyway, Hank.

HANK. What do you mean it didn't look that great?

MURIEL. It was squinchy in the armpits.

HANK. Why'd you let me buy a shirt looked squinchy in the armpits?

MURIEL. Because you seemed to like it.

HANK. I did like it but I wanted you to like the way I looked in it.

MURIEL. I hardly even noticed...

HANK. You hardly even noticed the way I looked!

MURIEL. No, the squinchiness! I hardly even noticed the squinchiness!

HANK. YOU should have bought me the presents anyway! I shouldn't have had to pick out my own presents! *(Hank hands the baby to Muriel, grabs a jacket, picks up a car battery, and heads for the door.)*

MURIEL. Where ya going, Hank?

HANK. I'm taking a sabbatical, I'm taking a leave of absence from my life! Gimme 24 hours to hear my brain think! Gimme 24 hours away from the smell of discount feet! Gimme 24 hours away from breasts that leak! Gimme 24 hours away from a baby with a snootful of tears! Gimme 24 hours a lung room! I got a necessity for lung room! If I don't get some lung room I'm gonna burst! *(He goes out the door. The door slams. The baby stops crying.)*

BLACKOUT

SCENE THREE

Trudi and Hank enter a motel room. There are some wan attempts at Christmas decoration — letters spelling Merry Christmas draped over the bed and some fuzzy gold garlands.

TRUDI. Oh.

HANK. What?

TRUDI. I can't stand it. I can't stand overhead light. It makes me depressed.

HANK. I'll turn out the light.

TRUDI. No. I have to see your face. Otherwise I get so alienated. I get so alienated right in the pit of my stomach.

HANK. I could get a lamp maybe. From the front desk.

TRUDI. I don't want you to leave. Ever since I saw that motel movie I can't be alone in a motel room. You know that scary one.

HANK. Which one?

TRUDI. The girl in the shower. Just thinking about it I get goose bumps. My nipples get erect.

Look at this. This gets me down. Foam pillows. I like feather. I'm one of those people squeeze my pillow which reveals a certain type of personality but at present I can't remember which type.

HANK. We don't have to stay here.

TRUDI. No, we do. You got a wife at your house and I'd take you to my house but I'm not ready for that. Then my house would remind me of you and if you dumped me my house would make me sad. *(Pause.)* You're supposed to say "I'm not gonna dump you."

HANK. I'm sorry. I wasn't listening.

TRUDI. I'm getting lonely being with you. The more I'm with you the lonelier I get. That's not a good sign. If I were older and wiser, I'd take a walk. I'd go home, watch "Miami Vice" and feel good about myself. I'd remind myself how good I live without a man. I'd regain my equilibrium. Ever since I met you, my life's been imbalanced, it tips in the love and sex direction. I look at your skin and think I'm gonna have a nervous breakdown if I'm not allowed to touch that man's skin. I meet 10 billion other men a day but I see you, my heart has a little heart attack, I get wet down there. Now then.

HANK. I'm sorry I made you feel lonely. My wife does that to me.

TRUDI. I figured maybe she did.

HANK. Winter's not a good time for her.

TRUDI. That's too bad 'cause up here that's half a person's life. You have a little heart attack when you see me?

HANK. When I see you I feel like I'm gonna cry. Because you're this person who wants me and I've been feeling like this thing nobody wants.

TRUDI. You're not a thing. You're a man.

HANK. I don't feel like a man.

TRUDI. You feel like a man to me, baby.

HANK. Call me that again. Baby. Call me nice names.

TRUDI. Baby. Sweetheart. Sugar. Punkin. Honey.

HANK. Your hair smells good.

TRUDI. Herbal Essence.

HANK. Yeah?

TRUDI. Yeah. Stop.

HANK. Why?

TRUDI. The overhead light. It's turning my skin green.

HANK. Close your eyes.

TRUDI. Hank.

HANK. I got a flashlight. I got a flashlight in my coat pocket. *(Hank digs up a flashlight. He hands it to Trudi who shines it in his face. Hank turns off the overhead light. The remainder of the scene is lit only by*

21

flashlight.)

TRUDI. I want to look at you. I want to memorize you for my old age. *(Pause.)*

HANK. Okay. Let me look at you now.

TRUDI. Don't look at my wrinkles.

HANK. Why not?

TRUDI. Hank?

HANK. Yeah.

TRUDI. I'm having a reality attack. I can't figure out who you are and where I am and how we came to be here. Say something. Soothe me. Console me. *(Hank turns off the flashlight and begins to kiss her. Lights fade to black.)*

SCENE FOUR

Later that night. Motel room.

TRUDI. Hank? That reality thing is happening again.

HANK. Aren't you sleepy?

TRUDI. Women don't go to sleep right after. It's different for women. It gets them stirred up.

HANK. Didn't you come?

TRUDI. That's not the issue, Hank. Trust me. The issue is I'm in bed with a man doesn't love me. How am I supposed to feel about that?

HANK. How do you know I don't love you?

TRUDI. I felt it when you kissed me.

HANK. I kissed you wrong.

TRUDI. When a man loves me he kisses me so tender I feel like crying.

HANK. I was too rough. I was too rough with you.

TRUDI. Sometimes when a man loves you he can be rough. It's like he can't forgive your body for being separate from his so he

22

bashes up against you like the collision could help the situation. But what I can't figure out is why some men adore you and others can take you or leave you. Or take you and leave you.

HANK. Or how somebody can love you and then stop loving you.

TRUDI. She ain't stopped loving you, Hank. It just got buried. She probably don't feel nothing for nobody right now. When a person's unhappy their heart goes dead.

HANK. She loves that baby.

TRUDI. Sure she loves the baby, a baby that young doesn't count as another person. It's like taking care of your arm, it's instinct. It's instinctual.

HANK. You have beautiful breasts.

TRUDI. Yeah.

HANK. You have beautiful skin.

TRUDI. Yeah.

HANK. Soft.

TRUDI. Yeah.

HANK. These are compliments. You're not supposed to say yeah to your own compliments.

TRUDI. Guys have said that stuff to me before so I'm used to it. Always they're talking about how soft my skin is so I figure it's true.

HANK. I love your teeth.

TRUDI. Come on.

HANK. I do.

TRUDI. They're crooked. I adopted a melancholy attitude to get out of smiling.

HANK. They make me want to run my tongue over them.

TRUDI. Yeah?

HANK. Anyone ever tell you that before?

TRUDI. No.

HANK. When I see your teeth suddenly I want to get bitten. I want you to bite me.

TRUDI. Bite you where?

HANK. On my ear. *(Trudi suddenly sits up.)*

TRUDI. Hank. It's that reality thing again. For a second you were my high school boyfriend. You were Scotty and I was 16 and you loved me. Scotty loved me. He stole money from the cash register at Gifford's ice cream parlor to buy me diamond earrings. He was a criminal for me, that's how much he loved me.

HANK. I wish I'd known you when you were 16.

TRUDI. I wish I was 16.

HANK. No you don't.

TRUDI. I do. I do.

HANK. What happened to Scotty?

TRUDI. I broke up with him. I broke up with him for another guy. Then I broke up with that guy for another guy and each time I thought I was getting closer to something I wanted but I was getting farther and farther away. Scotty wanted me to marry him but I said no way even though I was pregnant and coulda used the assistance. I had an abortion and after that I associated him with feeling so scared and doing something so bad.

HANK. You didn't do anything wrong, Trudi.

TRUDI. I did everything wrong. I did everything so wrong I got nobody to talk to but some stranger.

HANK. I'm not some stranger.

TRUDI. No?

HANK. No. I'm not a stranger and I'm not going anyplace. I'm gonna watch over you while you sleep. I'll be like an angel. Like your guardian angel.

TRUDI. Why don't she love you Hank? If you were mine I'd love you.

HANK. She used to love me. But then something happened.

TRUDI. What happened? What?

HANK. She overheard me tell this joke. It was down at the shoe outlet. She said it was a woman-hating joke and when the guys laughed it was evil man laughter. She said a man who loved a woman couldn't tell a joke like that. She said my love for her should carry over into my life with men.

TRUDI. What was the joke?

HANK. I don't want to tell you, it's not funny no more. It was a dirty joke, you know. There's been other stuff too. Like she's tired all the time with the baby and wants me to clean the house.

TRUDI. Do you?

HANK. I been meaning to, but like I don't know which stuff you use where. Like whether to use Top Job, Ajax, whatever. I used Lysol on the tub. She said that was incorrect so the hell with her.

TRUDI. Yeah, a tub needs an abrasive like Comet or Ajax, like that.

HANK. See? I don't know that stuff.

TRUDI. You could learn that stuff.

HANK. Look at it from my perspective. I work 40-50 hours a week down at the outlet. I'm doing my part.

TRUDI. But she doesn't feel you're doing your part.

HANK. No.

TRUDI. So you gotta respect her perspective.

HANK. What about my perspective? I gotta perspective too. Nobody respects my perspective.

TRUDI. Give and take you know.

HANK. When a woman says give and take, she means give and give and give some more. I know. I've heard that give and take stuff.

TRUDI. What about your sex life?

HANK. I can't discuss my sex life with you.

TRUDI. Why not? I'm part of it.

HANK. She says the doctor says no sex for 8 weeks after the baby's born. You believe that?

TRUDI. Sure I do. But if you're wondering about it, call the doctor. Say Muriel couldn't remember exactly what he said.

HANK. I can't do that. Let's say she's telling the truth.

TRUDI. Okay.

HANK. And the doctor said that to her.

TRUDI. Okay.

HANK. I think she's happy about it.

TRUDI. Oh.

BLACKOUT

25

SCENE FIVE

Hank sits, agitated, at the kitchen table. Muriel enters from outside with the baby and a diaper bag and a car battery. She sets the baby in the carriage and the battery by the stove.

HANK. Where you been?

MURIEL. Where you been?

HANK. I asked you first.

MURIEL. I stayed over your parents.

HANK. Why'd you stay over there? You got a house.

MURIEL. I was afraid you'd come home drunk or something.

HANK. Whattya mean come home drunk? This isn't Appalachia. Have I ever touched you? Have I ever even started to hit you?

MURIEL. No.

HANK. Then what is this? I'm your husband, you're acting like you're afraid of me.

MURIEL. I'm not afraid of you. But you're acting crazy.

HANK. How do you think you're acting?

MURIEL. I don't know, Hank, how am I acting?

HANK. You're acting miserable. I get miserable just looking at you. Last time I seen you smile was 1982.

MURIEL. Don't look at me if it makes you miserable.

HANK. I want to look at you. You're beautiful and I love to look at you but nobody looks back, even when your eyes look back nobody looks back. You're all abstracted, you're someplace else and I don't know where. You're like a pod person.

MURIEL. *(Looking around.)* This place is a dump. How long you been sitting here? You never once thought to pick up.

HANK. I thought about it.

MURIEL. I'll bet.

HANK. I thought about it but I was too aggravated to think about it. I was wondering where you were. I thought you were with a man.

MURIEL. What man?

HANK. Any man. A man with a college education.

MURIEL. Let me ask you something. Where would I find a man with a college education in this town?

HANK. The ski resort.

MURIEL. You thought I was with a skier with a college education.

HANK. It flashed before my eyes, yeah. 'Cause you were talking before about your college boyfriend read you Winnie-the-Pooh.

MURIEL. I didn't have any boyfriends in college.

HANK. Whattya mean you didn't have any boyfriends in college?

MURIEL. That's it, what you said, that's what I mean.

HANK. You were too picky maybe.

MURIEL. No one wanted me, Hank. I'm not beautiful. I wear glasses.

HANK. You are. You are beautiful.

MURIEL. What I have, Hank, is a smart face. So men think, I'll have a conversation with her then I'll go make love to the girl with the breasts.

HANK. What girl with the breasts?

MURIEL. Any girl with the breasts.

HANK. You got breasts.

MURIEL. Yeah, but they're just functional, you know.

HANK. You got beautiful breasts.

MURIEL. They're better now 'cause of the baby. But they leak.

HANK. I'm sorry I said that thing in mixed company about your

27

breasts leaking. It wasn't correct and they're not disgusting, I'm still adjusting that's all. Maybe you're still adjusting too and that's why you're shy about doing it with me.

MURIEL. I told you 100 times why not. Why not is 'cause the doctor said why not. Jesus Christ Hank, you got your elbow in sugar. Didn't it occur to you to grab a sponge and wipe it up? *(Muriel grabs a sponge and furiously starts cleaning.)*

HANK. No it didn't occur to me 'cause I was distraught.

MURIEL. You walk out on me and YOU'RE distraught.

HANK. I told you I'd be back. I told you I needed 24 hours.

MURIEL. What the hell is this?

HANK. It's a sink.

MURIEL. In the sink, what's in the sink?

HANK. Coffee grounds. I'll take care of it.

MURIEL. What, you're gonna buy me a new sink?

HANK. Whattya talking new sink? I just bought you a new sink.

MURIEL. How long have these grounds been in here?

HANK. Would you stop with the coffee grounds!

MURIEL. This will never come out.

HANK. Just use a little of the green stuff on it, the...

MURIEL. Comet! It's called Comet! Clean people use it to clean their houses! Men and women all over America use Comet to clean their houses!

HANK. Who's acting crazy now Muriel?

MURIEL. How many times have I told you to put the coffee grounds in the trash?

HANK. A couplea times, I forgot...

MURIEL. How many times have I told you I need some help running this house, I am not your maid I am a Magna Cum Laude graduate of the University of Maine Augusta. I change this baby twelve times a day, when she sleeps I stay awake with my ear tuned to a baby intercom. When she's hungry I get up and I feed her, when you're hungry I feed you and in between everybody's hunger I clean and I clean and I clean and this house still looks dark and dirty 'cause it's surrounded by totem poles! *(Muriel starts to get the baby's things together.)*

HANK. Where ya going?

MURIEL. Howard Johnson's motel where somebody else cleans the room!

HANK. This house is like a time-share vacation house. Nobody's ever here at the same time!

MURIEL. I'm gonna sample every ice cream flavor they got and put it all on your plastic! I'm gonna get fat and ugly and never grant you a divorce so you'll be stuck with this lumpen pajama person like I'm stuck with you! *(Muriel exits with the baby and the diaper bag. The second she's out the door, she re-enters, picks up her car battery and storms out.)*

INTERMISSION

SCENE SIX

Francine's trailer home. She is decorating a Christmas tree while Hank sits on a stepstool.

HANK. She took the baby and went to the Howard Johnson's. She's threatening to try every ice cream flavor before the night is through and put it all on my Visa card.

FRANCINE. She's at the motel or the restaurant?

HANK. Both. I didn't get to the cleaning like I promised so bam she's out the door, screaming about coffee grounds. This is no way to raise an infant baby, I'm telling you, an infantile baby, uprooting the baby to Hojos every time she's got a bug up her ass. The kid'll have nightmares, orange and blue nightmares. You know what she is, she's one of those anal personalties, got to have everything just so.

FRANCINE. Where were the coffee grounds?

HANK. In the sink. I dumped 'em in the sink 'til I could get to them. I didn't know they'd stain. The sink looks like a smoker's teeth. I don't know what to do, Ma, I don't know what to do.

FRANCINE. Why don't you clean the goddamn house like you promised?

HANK. Right. Exactly. Take her side. See it through her eyes. She's dropping a bundle at the Hojos, putting it on my plastic and she's the victim. I work 40 hours a week, what the hell does she do? She's been on vacation since 1932.

FRANCINE. She works 80 hours a week, bubba.

HANK. Bubba? Why'd you call me bubba? You're my mother. I should be more than some bubba to you.

FRANCINE. You used to be more than some bubba. Then you started acting like the rest of this town with the pick-up and the language and the girls.

HANK. What girls?

FRANCINE. The girl at the IGA. Happy Hours over at the Lobster Pot. What's her name? The girl with the chest.

HANK. I don't know her name.

FRANCINE. You know her name.

HANK. I don't know her name.

FRANCINE. Well you better know her name because if you slept with some girl and you don't even know her name you are a bigger bubba than I thought!

HANK. Trudi.

FRANCINE. Get rid of the girl, Hank. If Muriel doesn't know for sure she senses. You don't need a girl, you need a wife.

HANK. Tell that to Muriel.

FRANCINE. I'm telling you.

HANK. She hasn't been a wife to me. She hasn't been a wife to me for a long long time. She called me a Mister Man.

FRANCINE. Hmmmm. What does that mean?

HANK. That I'm just a guy, that I'm just this average guy.

FRANCINE. As opposed to what?

HANK. Someone special. I'm just not special in her eyes.

FRANCINE. It takes a special man to remain faithful to his wife.

HANK. I needed some sweetness in my life, Ma. Muriel she don't love me no more. I try to touch her at night, she turns away.

FRANCINE. Maybe she's tired. Maybe she's tired from the baby.

HANK. My house there's the crying and the diapers and the smell of milk boiling. My house has a disgusting smell. Trudi she wears this body lotion, this perfume lotion. Ciara. Like the wind. The wind in the desert.

FRANCINE. There's nothing wrong with the way your house smells. The way your house smells, Hank, your house smells like life.

HANK. Trudi she wears bras with birds sewn into the lace. A bird on each breast. And right where the beak is, that's where the nipple...

FRANCINE. When are you gonna name that baby?

HANK. I don't know. Muriel she has too many ideas and me I don't have any.

FRANCINE. A baby needs a name, Hank. There's something not right about a baby with no name. *(Dick enters carrying a large, brightly painted wooden butterfly.)*

DICK. Lookee here. Gotta truckload full of 'em.

HANK. What is it?

DICK. It's a butterfly.

HANK. What does it DO?

DICK. Doesn't do anything, that's the beauty of it. You nail 'em to your house, your mailbox, makes it distinctive.

HANK. You gonna sell them?

DICK. Nope. Gonna nail them onto the trailer, all one hundred and 37 of 'em. Quite a project.

HANK. Why are you spending your money on this shit?

DICK. I'll be good for giving directions. Turn right at the trailer with the butterflies.

HANK. Why are you spending your money on this shit?

DICK. *(Maine accent.)* My money.

HANK. You can't afford to spend thousands of dollars on knick-knacks.

31

DICK. You know what your problem is, son? You're not transcendent. You fail to see the spiritual power in things. Things diminish in your eyes. They expand in mine. *(Dick exits.)*

HANK. Dad's going insane.

FRANCINE. He's just retired with time on his hands, money on his hands.

HANK. How can he have money on his hands?

FRANCINE. You know, we saved. We planned to buy a real house but then I got used to the mobile home. I don't feel safe in a normal house. They're so wide. Anything can happen.

HANK. Why can't he just take up fishing or something?

FRANCINE. He won't eat fish. He won't eat meat anymore. He even apologizes to vegetables. If he's insane, I like it. He buys me those Whitman's samplers and takes out all the ones I don't like, according to the chart on the lid of the box. *(Hammering starts overhead.)*

HANK. The man's a fruitcake.

FRANCINE. He's a man with vision. He has a vision of how Life should be.

HANK. Yeah well I have a vision of how Life should be but Life isn't cooperating. My vision does not include a wife and child at the Howard Johnson's. It does not include a fruitcake father spending his savings on roadside souvenirs. Nor does it include a Mom calls me bubba.

FRANCINE. You want a good marriage, take a step towards a good marriage, you want your mother's love back, take a step towards getting your mother's love back. Do the right thing. Call up the girl, Hank, tell her it's over. *(Pause. The hammering stops.)*

HANK. I can't break up with her on the phone.

FRANCINE. Well you can't go see her.

HANK. Why not?

FRANCINE. One thing leads to another, her house, her bed, penetration.

HANK. I'll ask her could she stop by my house. Tonight.

FRANCINE. What about Muriel?

HANK. Muriel's at the Howard Johnson's.

FRANCINE. A woman's like an animal, she can sense another woman's been in her house. It's instinct.

HANK. I can't go to her house, she can't come to my house, I can't call her on the phone, what am I supposed to do?

FRANCINE. Write her a letter.

HANK. Okay but you gotta assist me 'cause I don't know how not to hurt a woman's feelings.

FRANCINE. Any woman goes with a married man is asking for pain pure and simple.

HANK. She's a fragile person. Lotta tragedy in her high school years. I don't want to contribute to her tragedy.

FRANCINE. Okay, get yourself a pad and pencil and we'll just sort of brainstorm. *(Hank gets a pad and pencil.)*

HANK. Dear Trudi. Vis à vis our intimacy.

FRANCINE. Hank, vis à vis is a business expression, it's not allowed in the world of romance.

HANK. See. Good. That's just the kind of assistance I require. That's just the kind of woman's point of view I'm looking for. Dear Trudi. You are a very nice girl. The nicest. The sweetest girl I met in a long time.

FRANCINE. Hank.

HANK. Yeah Ma?

FRANCINE. You're breaking up with her. That's like an ode.

HANK. Dear Trudi. You are in your house reading this letter on a different day from when I wrote it. Maybe I am dead by the time you get this, maybe you never got this letter and I am talking to myself.

FRANCINE. Hank.

HANK. Dear Trudi. My mother says I should make it up with Muriel and name my baby. Neither of these things involve you so good-bye. Hank.

FRANCINE. We need an adverb. How about "regretfully, Hank?"

HANK. I don't feel no regret.

FRANCINE. You don't feel any regret?

HANK. None whatsoever.

FRANCINE. What about Muriel?

HANK. Muriel never knew anything about it. We're like planets in separate orbits.

FRANCINE. So choose another adverb.

HANK. How about "Certainly" to indicate I am certain about what I gotta do.

FRANCINE. "Certainly, Hank?"

HANK. You gotta put it in context. Read the whole thing. Read it back to me.

FRANCINE. *(Reading.)* Dear Trudi. My mother says I should make it up with Muriel and name my baby. Neither of these things involve you so goodbye. Certainly, Hank.

HANK. It's no good. The whole thing is unacceptable. The truth is not always the best way to handle a situation. I can't break up with her in a letter, I got to see her in person, not only to do the tender thing but to prove to myself I can resist her particular temptations.

FRANCINE. The best way to resist temptation is to avoid temptation.

HANK. Ma, you helped me reach this decision, okay, but now I as a man have to implement this decision. This is what's gonna happen. I'm gonna go home. Muriel's gonna remain elsewhere. I'm gonna call Trudi on the phone, tell her come over I gotta talk with her, then I'm gonna tell her me and her we're a memory. I'm gonna kiss her softly and sweetly on the forehead. She's gonna return to her Life.

FRANCINE. Watch that softly and sweetly stuff.

HANK. Right Ma. I gotta go. *(Hank kisses his mother on the cheek then exits. She climbs up the stepstool.)*

FRANCINE. *(Calling after him.)* What if Muriel comes home?

HANK. *(Offstage.)* She won't come home. I know that woman like I know discount shoes! *(Crossfade.)*

SCENE SEVEN

Night. The kitchen. Hank enters. Trudi hovers in the doorway.

TRUDI. You sure it's okay?

HANK. Yeah yeah. Come on in.

TRUDI. I got beat up one time by a wife. She pulled my hair out. I had like a bald spot. I had to wear a fall. You know like on "I Dream of Jeanie."

HANK. You mean that wasn't her hair?

TRUDI. No that was a fall. They can match up your hair almost exactly. So exactly even you get confused.

HANK. By computer or something.

TRUDI. No, the naked eye. At least the place I went. Guy could do it just by looking.

HANK. *(Touching her hair.)* This is the real stuff though, right.

TRUDI. 100 percent.

HANK. Smells good.

TRUDI. Herbal Essence. I like natural products.

HANK. You should be on T.V.

TRUDI. Tell me about it. I could live for a year on one commercial.

HANK. You ever thought about doing that really?

TRUDI. Oh sure. Only thing is I got a crooked tooth. I meet a man can afford braces I'm gonna marry him. When I was little they called me snaggletooth. At least until I got breasts.

HANK. Then what'd they call you?

TRUDI. I would prefer not to say. Where's Muriel?

HANK. She's at the Howard Johnson's.

TRUDI. She went for ice cream?

HANK. Yes and no. She's temporarily left me.

TRUDI. She find out about me?

HANK. It was something else. It pertained to coffee grounds.

TRUDI. In the sink?

HANK. Yeah.

TRUDI. Something's been building up in her. A woman does not leave a man over coffee grounds less something's been building up in her. Did she have ambitions that got set aside when she married you?

HANK. She wanted to be something, yeah.

TRUDI. What?

HANK. That was it. That was as specific as it got. She wanted to be something. Trudi. How come you're being so nice about Muriel? Concerned even.

TRUDI. You know, what goes around comes around. *(Hank tears off a paper towel and gently hands it to Trudi.)*

HANK. Trudi. I can't come around no more.

TRUDI. Okay.

HANK. I'm breaking up with you.

TRUDI. Okay.

HANK. Okay. That's it? You're not rejected and sad and crumpled? You don't feel used and thrown away like a dirty Kleenex?

TRUDI. No. You have a one-sided perspective, Hank, that comes from living your whole life inside a certain perspective. Because at this time I could say to you don't you feel used by me, because everyone in the 20th century knows a woman can use a man sexually. Because she's lonely and maybe you're not up to her usual standards but it's winter and her feet get cold.

HANK. You slept with me 'cause your feet get cold?

TRUDI. It was a consideration.

HANK. You didn't love me?

TRUDI. Probably not.

HANK. But you said you did. When we did it you said I love you, I love you.

TRUDI. It was a part of my abandonment. I get abandoned in bed, I say things, I do things I wouldn't do any other time. And maybe at that moment I did love you Hank. You know like you are a dot on my time line.

HANK. I have no idea what you just said to me.

TRUDI. Okay. Like in history books they try to give you perspective. By showing a line and one dot is The Magna Carta and one dot is the Gutenberg Bible and another dot is The War of the Roses and another dot is Shakespeare's birth and another dot is...

HANK. All right.

TRUDI. Okay so I have this personal time line and you are a dot on my time line but even after we break up your dot is still there so at some point back there I am in the midst of loving you. I am in the midst of my abandonment.

HANK. Weren't you ever jealous? Didn't you ever think what if I left Muriel and married you?

TRUDI. Frankly?

HANK. Yeah.

TRUDI. No. I mean, who wants to marry a guy cheats on his wife? Muriel's in it for the long haul. I'm just part of the ebb and flow of your married life. I recognize that. I recognize that and accept it. Muriel has a claim on you. I make no such claim. This is the difference between me and some women. I just use married men as a resource.

HANK. You never wanted to marry me?

TRUDI. If people wanted to marry everyone they slept with life would get confusing.

HANK. I wanted to marry everyone I ever slept with. I get tender. I feel tender towards them. I want to take care of them. A new person sees you different. So each new person is a chance to be a new person.

TRUDI. You thought about getting married to me?

HANK. Yeah.

TRUDI. No, really.

HANK. Yeah.

TRUDI. Yeah?

HANK. Yeah.

TRUDI. *(Touching his lips.)* I like this mouth.

HANK. Trudi.

TRUDI. What we have here is a mouth situation.

HANK. *(Pushing her hand away.)* No.

TRUDI. Why not?

HANK. I'm breaking up with you.

TRUDI. Besides that.

HANK. I can't do it in her house. I'm one person with you. I'm another person here.

TRUDI. You're the same person. You're the same person. I want to kiss this person good-bye. *(Trudi and Hank kiss. Muriel enters carrying the baby. She sees them, registers it and walks back out. Beat. Trudi and Hank look at each other. Muriel re-enters.)*

MURIEL. You, tits. I want you out of here.

TRUDI. My name is Trudi.

MURIEL. How do you do. Get the fuck out of my house. *(Trudi exits. Hank furiously begins to scrub the sink. He tapers off and looks at Muriel.)* You are so in the wrong. You have done something so incorrect.

HANK. I was breaking it off with her.

MURIEL. You obviously weren't being real firm about that, Hank, her tongue was down your throat.

HANK. She wanted to kiss me good-bye.

MURIEL. Kiss me good-bye baby, 'cause I'm outta here.

HANK. Where you going?

MURIEL. Where I am going, you cannot follow. Even standing here right now I am so far away from you, you can't afford the bus fare.

HANK. You didn't love me no more, I tried to tell you, one look from you would have been worth more to me than...

MURIEL. You insult me. You insult everything I am by choosing my opposite.

HANK. You looked at me like I wasn't here, like in your head you'd already left me. The baby cries when I try to hold her, and when I try to hold you, you move away like I got cold hands. *(Muriel heads for the door.)* IT'S SNOWING OUT THERE! You'll skid, you'll die, I'll never see you again. I'll never see the baby again. I'll be in a dark suit following two coffins to the grave, ladies in veils will hand me tissues.

MURIEL. Okay. I'll stay. You get out. I'm the fucking injured party, you get out.

HANK. The stove's gone out, you and the baby will freeze to death. I'll be in a dark suit following two coffins to the grave, oh I can't stand it. I'm going out for some wood.

MURIEL. Don't bother.

HANK. I'm going out for some wood. You can reject me. You can turn on me. You can wash your hands of me. But this is still my family. It's like a primordial thing. I'm like a dinosaur with this giant dinosaur instinct drive! My house is cold. My family is cold. I'm going foraging. I'm going out for some wood.

MURIEL. Mr. Wilk hasn't dropped off the new cord yet.

HANK. I don't need an official cord of wood. I don't need regulation firewood. I am a man with primordial urges!

MURIEL. You could do with a few less primordial urges, buddy.

HANK. Yeah right Muriel, stick the knife in and twist it. I bring you my shame. I have deposited my shame at your feet and still you torment me.

MURIEL. Your shame.

HANK. Right.

MURIEL. You've deposited your shame at my feet?

HANK. Yeah.

MURIEL. BIG DEAL! I don't want your shame. I can't use your shame. I can't frame your shame and put it up on my wall. I can't cook your shame and eat it for breakfast. I can't bottle your shame and dab it behind my ears. Your shame means nothing to me. All I have is the hurt inside me that the one person on this Earth supposed to love me more than Life itself has spit on me, called me ugly...

HANK. I never...

MURIEL. YOU CALLED ME UGLY WITH YOUR AC-
TIONS! How can I compete with that Hank? *(Muriel gestures to the
door, meaning Trudi.)* Those ... limbs. That skin. She's golden
brown in the middle of winter, like a marshmallow toasted just
right. She's like, me upside down, big tits and no hips, no varicose
veins, no cellulite...
HANK. She got cellulite.
MURIEL. She does?
HANK. Like when she crosses her legs or something you see it
ripple or...
MURIEL. DON'T DISTRACT ME! DON'T DISTRACT
ME FROM MY RAGE! *(Pause, then Hank suddenly grabs the ax and
goes out the door.)*

BLACKOUT

SCENE EIGHT

*Francine is holding the baby and looking out the window.
Muriel is racing around the kitchen throwing strange things into
her suitcase like egg timers and pot holders.*

FRANCINE. I thought <u>he</u> was gonna go and you were gonna
stay.
MURIEL. I changed my mind. These boots were made for walking, blizzard or no blizzard. I'm gonna be in a urban environment by
daybreak. Fuck nature. Fuck the country. I'd sell this house for
green stamps.
FRANCINE. What's he doing out there?
MURIEL. He's chopping 'em down. He's chopping 'em down
for firewood, figures there's a good cord of wood out there.
FRANCINE. He's in his bare feet.
MURIEL. WHAT?

FRANCINE. See for yourself.

MURIEL. *(Opening the storm door.)* IT'S SNOWING YOU ASSHOLE! *(She shuts the door.)* Asshole. Doesn't have the sense God gave a chicken. What a loser. What a loser that man is.

FRANCINE. What you have is a tempestous relationship. Alot of people would give their right arm for a tempestuous relationship. What he's been doing he's been doing to get your attention.

MURIEL. What he's been doing is dipping his wick.

FRANCINE. It happens.

MURIEL. Not to me it doesn't. I'm not one of the girls. I don't stand in line. I am a remarkable woman.

FRANCINE. You know what this is like? This is like those movies when two lovers are drifting away from each other and the audience knows they've got it all wrong, that really they love each other. Like on my soap opera a woman left her husband to live with another man but really she did it to protect her husband from the man who was a gangster.

MURIEL. There's no hidden agenda here. The man stepped out on me, while I was home mourning the loss of my thighs. I lost my figure bearing a child for that man.

FRANCINE. What about the baby? The baby needs a father.

MURIEL. I'll find her another one.

FRANCINE. Now you're just being a wiseacre. If you would look out this window the wisecracks would stop. If you would look out this window your heart would break.

MURIEL. I'm gonna be something. I'm not gonna waste my life in this mosquito pit.

FRANCINE. What are you gonna be?

MURIEL. Something. I'm gonna move to New York City and buy the right clothes. There'll be a sadness in me no man can touch. Ah, Francine you shoulda seen that motel. So clean I would like to a lived there and conveniences — Kleenexes coming out of the walls, little packages of mouthwash, Whispermint, like candy only good for you, in the shower a dispenser full of Eurobath with glycerine you can use it anywhere, hands, face, hair whatever, and on the T.V. a little paper tent, a questionnaire asking me was I satisfied,

41

the first time in my life anyone ever asked me.

FRANCINE. So why'd you come home?

MURIEL. EXACTLY.

HANK. *(Outside, drawing closer.)* MURIEL! MURIEL!

MURIEL. Take the baby. Go out the front way.

FRANCINE. What are you gonna do?

MURIEL. I'll meet you at your house. I gotta clean the sink.

FRANCINE. Now? *(Muriel grabs a can of Comet and begins to clean the sink furiously. Francine hurries out with the baby. Hank is screaming Muriel's name outside, coming closer and closer. Muriel yells outside to Hank while scrubbing the sink.)*

MURIEL. Save your breath, Hank, 'cause I'm not gonna reconcile with you! I don't care if you chop down every totem pole in the state of Maine! Your primordial insanity got nothing to do with me personally, with me as a person. Things were bad and getting badder long before I walked in this house tonight and I don't even care I promised God I'd love and honor you 'cause I don't honor you no more. You've lost your honor in my eyes, you're not an honorable man! There is nothing there is nada there is zero there is goose egg you could possibly say to me to make me reconcile with you! *(Hank appears outside carrying an armload of chopped up totem poles. He yells into the kitchen.)*

HANK. I cut off my toe for you. On purpose. I cut off my toe for you on purpose. *(Muriel steps outside and looks at him.)* I wanted to be an artist for you. I wanted to suffer for you. I wanted to hurt like I made you hurt. I wanted you to take me back. Take me back. *(Hank drops the load in the snow and holds out his arms to her. Muriel lets out a sob. She drops the Comet and sponge and runs to him. She jumps on him, straddling her legs around his hips as he twirls around. At that moment, across stage, the trailer blazes with light. The large wooden butterflies that cover the trailer are draped with Christmas tree white lights. Angels with trumpets are perched on the corners of the roof, spouting carols from speakers Dick has rigged up. Hank sees the trailer lit up.)* Muriel! Behold! Behold Muriel! *(Hank falls to his knees and pulls Muriel down beside him.)* Millions of butterflies bejeweled bedecked taking wing while angels play their triumphorous sounds!

MURIEL. Hank, that's your Mom and Dad's trailer what with the Christmas decorations and all.

HANK. Yes! It is! It is! It is THAT and MORE, it is a thing in and of itself and it is another thing, a thing greater than the thing it is! Muriel, I'm having an experience, I'm experiencing an experience, I'm so glad you're here to experience it with me!

MURIEL. Hank? You lose alot of blood?

HANK. I didn't lose it. I know just where it is.

MURIEL. Does it hurt?

HANK. I think my stump is frozen, it's like novocained.

MURIEL. *(Getting up.)* We gotta get you to the hospital.

HANK. No!

MURIEL. If we go to the hospital soon they can sew your toe back on.

HANK. I want to SUFFER for you!

MURIEL. You'll still have the scar. The scar from where you chopped it off.

HANK. I don't think it's correct to renege on my suffering.

MURIEL. Hank.

HANK. Are you saying I should put the toe back on for your sake?

MURIEL. Yes.

HANK. For your sake I will do so. Only one thing.

MURIEL. What?

HANK. I've misplaced my toe.

MURIEL. WHAT?

HANK. In the snow. I misplaced my toe in the snow.

MURIEL. Well we have to FIND it. *(Starting to search.)* Your tracks are covered, Hank, the blood's all covered.

HANK. *(Starting to search.)* I was in front of the totem pole looks like you. It was an offering to a shrine kind of thing. That was my logic.

MURIEL. Hank?

HANK. Yeah Muriel?

MURIEL. How many times were you with her?

HANK. Muriel. Keep looking, Muriel.

43

MURIEL. Did you do it in a car?

HANK. The toe, Muriel, the toe!

MURIEL. Did you do it at her house?

HANK. I never saw her house.

MURIEL. Did you do it at our house?!

HANK. A motel, a motel! It was ugly! There was ... carpeting.

MURIEL. Did you tell her about me?

HANK. *(Pleading.)* Muriel...

MURIEL. Did you tell her about me?

HANK. I don't know which is the right answer!

MURIEL. You didn't tell her about me?!

HANK. Yes! I did!

MURIEL. You TOLD her about me?!

HANK. No! Yes! I told her! I couldn't stop telling her! I was lovesick during my whole affair. I was lovesick for you, Muriel!

MURIEL. You were!

HANK. I was lovesick all over my body! *(They embrace.)* Muriel! I got an idea, Muriel! I got an idea sends shivers up my spine! My idea is this. You know like chickens, you cut off their head, they run around. What about the head? What happens to the head? Does it think thoughts? I'm thinking if I were my toe where would I go? I think my toe went to the hospital. If my toe was thinking it would have gone to the hospital!

BLACKOUT

SCENE NINE

Hank is on the phone with his father. Muriel is holding the baby and yelling her version of the events.

HANK. My toe was in the parking lot. I think it pooped out or it woulda gone all the way to the emergency room.

MURIEL. They think maybe that wasn't his toe!

44

HANK. Garbage. It was a perfect fit, it was like a jigsaw puzzle that toe.

MURIEL. They think maybe it fell out of an ambulance! They think it was somebody else's toe.

HANK. Well it's my toe now. You know what their problem is those doctors? They're not transcendent. They don't acknowledge the miraculous. I say something's bigger than me, so be it. Now? We're just hanging around waiting for the turkey. That'd be great, Dad. Okay, we'll see you in a minute. *(Hank hangs up the phone.)* They're stopping by on the way to the Christmas pageant to drop off the baby's presents. What do you think, we need another log? This totem pole wood burns beautiful.

MURIEL. Really goes, huh?

HANK. Oh yeah. What's that smell? Flowers or something. I smell flowers in the winter!

MURIEL. Perfume, Hank. I'm wearing perfume.

HANK. You're wearing perfume?

MURIEL. Yeah.

HANK. For me.

MURIEL. *(Shyly.)* Yeah.

HANK. Come here. Let me smell. *(He nuzzles her neck.)* O, I love that place. I wish I could be a hickey or something. Live between your ear and your shoulder. Your earrings would dangle on me. I'd feel your breath when you sighed. *(The baby gurgles.)* She's giggling at me this baby. *(Muriel gives Hank the baby to hold.)* Who's giggling me? Who's giggling me? Muriel. A name flashed before my eyes. A hybrid name like two flowers joined together. Your name and my name. Together.

MURIEL. Murank?

HANK. No, my real name. Henry.

MURIEL. Murry.

HANK. No. Henriel.

MURIEL. Henriel?

HANK and MURIEL. *(Softly.)* Henriel. *(Sound of carolers singing "What Child is This?" outside.)*

HANK. Hark. I like this song. What's this song?

MURIEL. "What Child is This."

HANK. I thought it was "Greensleeves."

MURIEL. No. "What Child is This." Must be the group from First Baptist.

HANK. I don't think so. I think they're angels.

MURIEL. What makes you think they're angels?

HANK. Listen to them. Nobody around here sings that good. *(Hank and Muriel look into the baby carriage, listening to the carol. Dick and Francine enter across stage, dressed for the Christmas pageant, as the Three Kings of Orient Are. They wear crowns and ermine-trimmed red robes. They carry shopping bags full of presents, one princess doll with a crown, and they pull a toy donkey on wheels. They move slowly across the stage towards Hank and Muriel.)*

FRANCINE. *(Practicing.)* For we have seen his star in the East... *(Francine turns to Dick, hopefully. He cannot remember his line.)*

HANK. Hey Muriel?

MURIEL. Yeah Hank?

HANK. I got a good feeling about this.

END OF PLAY

PROPERTY LIST

KITCHEN AREA
Small round kitchen table with table cloth
Muriel's poached eggs set Upstage on table
Hank's poached eggs set Stage Left on table
4 wooden kitchen chairs set around the table
Hank's tan pants hung over the back of the Down Stage chair
Kitchen sink with running water
Coffee grounds in a coffee filter in the sink
Preset on the counter around the sink:

       Container of Comet

       Dish drainer with dishes in it

       4 sponges

       Francine's cigarettes with a saucer for an ashtray
Refrigerator Upstage Right in kitchen
Large box of tissues on top of refrigerator
Stack of bills and receipts on top of refrigerator
Inside refrigerator:

       1 half full quart of milk

       Apple

       4 bottles of baby formula
Telephone hanging on kitchen wall Stage Right of door
Kitchen door closed
Curtains on the window pulled open
Sideboard Upstage below the kitchen window
On top of sideboard:

       Car battery

       Flashlight
Inside of sideboard:

       Box of bills and receipts

       Muriel's baby name book

Woodstove Stage Left in kitchen
Woodbasket Downstage of woodstove
Ax in woodbasket
Kindling in woodbasket
Water spilled on floor Stage Left of table

MOTEL AREA
Bed with a sheet
Motel chair and end table

TRAILER HOME AREA
Christmas tree
Christmas ornaments
Pad and pencil

OFF STAGE PRESET
Party hats
4 plates with birthday cake
2 cups for coffee
Toaster
Baby
Bag with baby's things in it
Head of a totem pole
Dick's wooden butterfly

COSTUME PLOT

MURIEL
Scene 1

>White nightgown
>Blue bedroom slippers
>Blue sweatshirt

Scene 2

>Blue/grey flannel shirt
>Olive drab skirt
>Navy cardigan sweater

Scene 4

>Blue turtleneck
>Red & black plaid shirt

Scene 7

>Jeans
>Green down vest
>Blue knit hat
>L.L. Bean boots
>White nightgown

Scene 9

>Blue robe

HANK
Scene 1

>Beige chinos
>Red sweater
>White shirt
>Tan boots
>Boxer shorts
>Red socks

Scene 8
>White undershirt
>Torn and bloodied double for undershirt

Scene 9
>Brown bathrobe

TRUDI

Scene 3
>Rabbit fur jacket
>Pink sweater
>Pale denim skirt
>Lace hose
>Pink lacey camisole
>Bra
>Jewelry
>Pink scarf

Scene 7
>White sweater with buttons
>Beige miniskirt
>Short beige boots
>Ear muffs
>Beige handbag

FRANCINE

Scene 2
>Blue jeans
>White sweater
>Wool socks
>Work boots

Scene 6
>Cream flannel plaid shirt
>Red sweat pants

Scene 8
>Turquoise parka
>Black moccasin slippers

Scene 9

> Purple king's robe
> White towel for headwrap
> Crown

DICK
Scene 2

> Green work pants
> Red/blue flannel shirt
> Black suspenders
> Yellow rain slicker
> Black snow boots
> Wool socks
> Dark gray fedora

Scene 6

> Green quilted vest
> Denim overalls
> Fedora

Scene 9

> Orange king's robe
> White towel as headwrap
> Crown

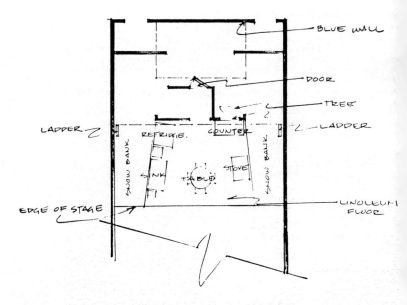

BLUE WALL

DOOR

TREE

LADDER

LADDER

REFRIDGE.

COUNTER

SNOW BANK

SNOW BANK

SINK

STOVE

TABLE

EDGE OF STAGE

LINOLEUM FLOOR

DOTTED LINE SHOWS UPPER LEVEL

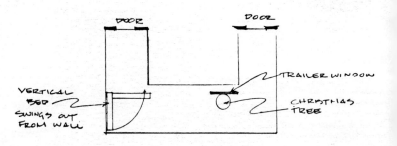

DOOR

DOOR

TRAILER WINDOW

VERTICAL BED SWINGS OUT FROM WALL

CHRISTMAS TREE

UPPER LEVEL

SCENE DESIGN
"APOCALYPTIC BUTTERFLIES"
Designed by Nephelie Andonyadis for
New Arts Theatre

NEW PLAYS

★ **BE AGGRESSIVE by Annie Weisman.** Vista Del Sol is paradise, sandy beaches, avocado-lined streets. But for seventeen-year-old cheerleader Laura, everything changes when her mother is killed in a car crash, and she embarks on a journey to the Spirit Institute of the South where she can learn "cheer" with Bible belt intensity. "...filled with lingual gymnastics...stylized rapid-fire dialogue..." –*Variety*. "...a new, exciting, and unique voice in the American theatre..." –*BackStage West*. [1M, 4W, extras] ISBN: 0-8222-1894-1

★ **FOUR by Christopher Shinn.** Four people struggle desperately to connect in this quiet, sophisticated, moving drama. "...smart, broken-hearted...Mr. Shinn has a precocious and forgiving sense of how power shifts in the game of sexual pursuit...He promises to be a playwright to reckon with..." –*NY Times*. "A voice emerges from an American place. It's got humor, sadness and a fresh and touching rhythm that tell of the loneliness and secrets of life...[a] poetic, haunting play." –*NY Post*. [3M, 1W] ISBN: 0-8222-1850-X

★ **WONDER OF THE WORLD by David Lindsay-Abaire.** A madcap picaresque involving Niagara Falls, a lonely tour-boat captain, a pair of bickering private detectives and a husband's dirty little secret. "Exceedingly whimsical and playfully wicked. Winning and genial. A top-drawer production." –*NY Times*. "Full frontal lunacy is on display. A most assuredly fresh and hilarious tragicomedy of marital discord run amok...absolutely hysterical..." –*Variety*. [3M, 4W (doubling)] ISBN: 0-8222-1863-1

★ **QED by Peter Parnell.** Nobel Prize-winning physicist and all-around genius Richard Feynman holds forth with captivating wit and wisdom in this fascinating biographical play that originally starred Alan Alda. "QED is a seductive mix of science, human affections, moral courage, and comic eccentricity. It reflects on, among other things, death, the absence of God, travel to an unexplored country, the pleasures of drumming, and the need to know and understand." –*NY Magazine*. "Its rhythms correspond to the way that people—even geniuses—approach and avoid highly emotional issues, and it portrays Feynman with affection and awe." –*The New Yorker*. [1M, 1W] ISBN: 0-8222-1924-7

★ **UNWRAP YOUR CANDY by Doug Wright.** Alternately chilling and hilarious, this deliciously macabre collection of four bedtime tales for adults is guaranteed to keep you awake for nights on end. "Engaging and intellectually satisfying...a treat to watch." –*NY Times*. "Fiendishly clever. Mordantly funny and chilling. Doug Wright teases, freezes and zaps us." –*Village Voice*. "Four bite-size plays that bite back." –*Variety*. [flexible casting] ISBN: 0-8222-1871-2

★ **FURTHER THAN THE FURTHEST THING by Zinnie Harris.** On a remote island in the middle of the Atlantic secrets are buried. When the outside world comes calling, the islanders find their world blown apart from the inside as well as beyond. "Harris winningly produces an intimate and poetic, as well as political, family saga." –*Independent (London)*. "Harris' enthralling adventure of a play marks a departure from stale, well-furrowed theatrical terrain." –*Evening Standard (London)*. [3M, 2W] ISBN: 0-8222-1874-7

★ **THE DESIGNATED MOURNER by Wallace Shawn.** The story of three people living in a country where what sort of books people like to read and how they choose to amuse themselves becomes both firmly personal and unexpectedly entangled with questions of survival. "This is a playwright who does not just tell you what it is like to be arrested at night by goons or to fall morally apart and become an aimless yet weirdly contented ghost yourself. He has the originality to make you feel it." –*Times (London)*. "A fascinating play with beautiful passages of writing..." –*Variety*. [2M, 1W] ISBN: 0-8222-1848-8

DRAMATISTS PLAY SERVICE, INC.
440 Park Avenue South, New York, NY 10016 212-683-8960 Fax 212-213-1539
postmaster@dramatists.com www.dramatists.com

NEW PLAYS

★ **SHEL'S SHORTS by Shel Silverstein.** Lauded poet, songwriter and author of children books, the incomparable Shel Silverstein's short plays are deeply infused with the sam wicked sense of humor that made him famous. "…[a] childlike honesty and twisted sens of humor." –*Boston Herald.* "…terse dialogue and an absurdity laced with a tang of drea give [*Shel's Shorts*] more than a trace of Samuel Beckett's comic existentialism." –*Bosto Phoenix.* [flexible casting] ISBN: 0-8222-1897-6

★ **AN ADULT EVENING OF SHEL SILVERSTEIN by Shel Silverstein.** Welcome t the darkly comic world of Shel Silverstein, a world where nothing is as it seems and wher the most innocent conversation can turn menacing in an instant. These ten imaginativ plays vary widely in content, but the style is unmistakable. "…[*An Adult Evening*] show off Silverstein's virtuosic gift for wordplay…[and] sends the audience out…with a clea appreciation of human nature as perverse and laughable." –*NY Times.* [flexible casting] ISBN: 0-8222-1873-9

★ **WHERE'S MY MONEY? by John Patrick Shanley.** A caustic and sardonic vivisection of the institution of marriage, laced with the author's inimitable razor-sharp wit "…Shanley's gift for acid-laced one-liners and emotionally tumescent exchanges is certainly potent…" –*Variety.* "…lively, smart, occasionally scary and rich in reverse wisdom." –*NY Times.* [3M, 3W] ISBN: 0-8222-1865-8

★ **A FEW STOUT INDIVIDUALS by John Guare.** A wonderfully screwy comedy-drama that figures Ulysses S. Grant in the throes of writing his memoirs, surrounded by a cast of fantastical characters, including the Emperor and Empress of Japan, the opera star Adelina Patti and Mark Twain. "Guare's smarts, passion and creativity skyrocket to awesome heights…" –*Star Ledger.* "…precisely the kind of good new play that you might call an everyday miracle…every minute of it is fresh and newly alive…" –*Village Voice.* [10M, 3W] ISBN: 0-8222-1907-7

★ **BREATH, BOOM by Kia Corthron.** A look at fourteen years in the life of Prix, a Bronx native, from her ruthless girl-gang leadership at sixteen through her coming to maturity at thirty. "…vivid world, believable and eye-opening, a place worthy of a dramatic visit, where no one would want to live but many have to." –*NY Times.* "…rich with humor, terse vernacular strength and gritty detail…" –*Variety.* [1M, 9W] ISBN: 0-8222-1849-6

★ **THE LATE HENRY MOSS by Sam Shepard.** Two antagonistic brothers, Ray and Earl, are brought together after their father, Henry Moss, is found dead in his seedy New Mexico home in this classic Shepard tale. "…His singular gift has been for building mysteries out of the ordinary ingredients of American family life…" –*NY Times.* "…rich moments …Shepard finds gold." –*LA Times.* [7M, 1W] ISBN: 0-8222-1858-5

★ **THE CARPETBAGGER'S CHILDREN by Horton Foote.** One family's history spanning from the Civil War to WWII is recounted by three sisters in evocative, intertwining monologues. "…bittersweet music—[a] rhapsody of ambivalence…in its modest, garrulous way…theatrically daring." –*The New Yorker.* [3W] ISBN: 0-8222-1843-7

★ **THE NINA VARIATIONS by Steven Dietz.** In this funny, fierce and heartbreaking homage to *The Seagull*, Dietz puts Chekhov's star-crossed lovers in a room and doesn't let them out. "A perfect little jewel of a play…" –*Shepherdstown Chronicle.* "…a delightful revelation of a writer at play; and also an odd, haunting, moving theater piece of lingering beauty." –*Eastside Journal (Seattle).* [1M, 1W (flexible casting)] ISBN: 0-8222-1891-7

DRAMATISTS PLAY SERVICE, INC.
440 Park Avenue South, New York, NY 10016 212-683-8960 Fax 212-213-1539
postmaster@dramatists.com www.dramatists.com